With *Now in Contest* Richa[...] essential voices.

Martin Buber said, "We can be redeemed only to the extent to which we see ourselves." Elusive redemption, hinged on the unending struggle to recognize our neighbors truthfully—that's at the core of Levine's vision. His poems are "I-Thou" to the marrow—which, in America, means they tackle war, racism, climate privilege. Levine speaks with Whitmanesque directness (though perhaps not Whitmanesque optimism) to the reader, to Buddy Holley, to a student in Bushwick. His voice can bridge unfathomable distances: "[f]or you and me, / it goes back to Quang Tri and a wet / mortar round that fell short of the LZ, / killed you and left me with a deadness/in the right ear..."

Richard Levine refuses to allow our violent culture to be a spectacle. He takes the risk of living it. *Now in Contest* is a book I will treasure and return to.

D. Nurkse

author of *Love in the Last Days: After Tristan and Iseult* and *A Night in Brooklyn*

From "the bellows of cows / barn-bred and lamenting their exile from the wild" to the slow "intravenous drip" of time, from a "morning image of flesh / and good fortune" to "this heaven of quiet hope," Richard Levine's poems range far and wide across a landscape that encompasses war and holocaust, class and race, inner city teaching and rural rejuvenation, love of nature and fear for its survival. Levine has a heart as big as the sky and the gift of words to convey it.

W. D. Ehrhart

author of *Thank You for Your Service: Collected Poems*

"A wood, like a poem,
turns and turns: enchanted and real,
dream and waking, musical and mute,"

The poems in Richard Levine's *Now in Contest* arrive with an icy hit; they offer wistful beginnings and awful endings. They are both brutal and tender, bitter and loving, as in "Where Chemistry Fails": "he [Primo Levi] never stopped loving the way chemistry could explain how / things are made—" Levine takes the reader from childhood memories of relatives' war to his own terrible Vietnam, as in "Memorial Day": "I carry your death shrouded / in that wish..." His images move from a tenuous dark to those moments of the teacher he was: "O my breathless wards," he says, and the reader wishes to be one of his lucky students. Levine is a master of his craft; his strong voice offers experience like a gift, shares "the promise of warm seasons / that come and go on wings."

Bertha Rogers
author of *Wild, Again*

Now in Contest

Richard Levine

Fernwood
PRESS

Now in Contest

Fernwood Press
Newberg, Oregon
www.fernwoodpress.com

Printed in the United States of America

Cover photo: Richard Levine

ISBN 978-1-59498-098-5

"Two opposing laws seem to me now in contest. The one, a law of blood and death, opening out each day new modes of destruction, forces nations to be always ready for battle. The other, a law of peace, work and health, whose only aim is to deliver man from the calamities which beset him. The one seeks violent conquests, the other the relief of mankind. The one places a single life above all victories, the other sacrifices hundreds of thousands of lives to the ambition of a single individual."

—Louis Pasteur

"... shall we not best guide humanity by telling the truth about all this, so far as the truth is ascertainable?"

—W. E. B. DuBois

to Soraya Hadassah Levine-Brooks,
in affectionate commemoration Sheila Yates and Martha Speer

Contents

Cover Letter

Dear Reader,

We must be changing, adapting or evolving in significant ways, in order to live with Covid confinement, the effects of a wooden cross being driven into the heart of American democracy, the zero-sum economy, the black & white ballistics of social justice and racial inequality, the sport of mass-shootings as political discourse, the relentless genocidal assault on Ukraine and on less publicized black and brown nations, and industry's death-wish denial of an imminent climate holocaust. It's made loved ones ever more important, and yet some days it is something as small and selfish as eating a candy bar in the solitude of my parked car that makes the day bearable. And one question that writing poses is whether to grieve over our collective witness of real human suffering and our capacity to inflict it, or, beyond the reach of algorithmic targeting, to horde and huddle alone with some small confection.

There might be more that I could do than to scrawl these poems day after day, trying to tell some small self-evident truths about what is now in contest. But until I discover how I might be more useful, I work like a graffiti or mural artist at the top of a fragile scaffold, brushing my perceptions of the world on the blank sides of buildings for all who might look to see. Then, I clean my brushes and go home to my wife.

Peace,

Richard Levine,
Brooklyn, NY
May 2022

The Law of Blood and Death

"I know not with what weapons World War III will be fought, but World War IV will be fought with sticks and stones."

—Albert Einstein

One Night in America

The first time I noticed my hands
trembling, I was still a young man,
just returned from a war, and even
pressing palms and all ten fingers
against a windowpane to steady them,

I knew that like slither-quick rodent-
eating snakes in swamp-black water
or a sudden shiver in the hang
of moss, it would always be there,
that fear, quaking in each next step,
ready to pounce and remind me.

So to those now walking war's trails—
I hope you survive the war and the coming home,
especially you young Black veterans,
pulled over one night in America,
white policemen pointing their flashlights
in your window.

Wade in the Water

For an angel went down at a certain season into the pool,
*   and troubled the water.*
*   (John 5:4)*

I can't immunize you with my nod
or smile, passing in this pig-pink
rural town, where your skin
is as double-take out-of-place
as the blood-colored tears
on a waxwing's shoulders.

And you don't need protection to walk
here, nor anyone's approval. But you know,
easy as catching a cold or rain on cloudy days,
a chance of hate might be in your forecast
anywhere you go. And even if justice shines
on your back door someday, we'll still need
an umbrella for that rain that falls on only one side
of a street, like a wall with loneliness on both.

Every Day, You Say

You say you won't report the store
or the security guard that followed you
down every aisle.

You say you don't want to be the cause
of a march or the name a Supreme Court case
is known by.

You say, I just don't get it, that I don't
understand: it's about the hurt. Every day.
Every day, you say, it's about the hurt.

Immigrant

My mother's father's name was Isadore.
Being a prodigal punster, I'd ask
and shout, "Grandpa is a door?!"

He'd laugh, tousle my hair, not
understanding a single word. We never spoke,
being far in tongue as Brooklyn

from brutal Svislach, where he was a boy
and hunted as a Jew. Doors closed before
I knew him, by the nostril pinch

of pipe tobacco in his flannel and gabardine
clothes and the dry-lipped kisses he was stingy with.
At corners, he took my hand in his

smooth-skinned baker's grip—strong, insistent,
and brave as his resolve at midnight border crossings.

Bahbe

What made her so cold, so distant—
never hugging, never touching,
except in posed photographs. Even then
she needed to be told—move closer,
put your arm around his shoulder.

Was it something in the Russian
folk songs she hummed, but never taught?
Did she know the words? Did she sing
them to her children, lullaby
my mother to sleep with them?

What made her so cold, so distant—
was it the consonant-hard hatred
and hunting of Jews, the famines?
How I longed for signs of her love,
that woman I never saw smile.

Fat Pickers

for Manya Goldberg

Your mother sent you out at dusk
to pick fat from garbage cans.
You wrapped it in newspaper.

The fat-loosened letters and words,
smudged beyond legibility, slipped
from the page. You didn't care
what they said or where they went.
News could not satisfy hunger.

Your mother mustered a thin, gray-
water broth from the fat. Dissolved,
it floated like blisters oozing yellow pus.

Neither that nor an errant swirl of ink
stopped you from drinking it before it
cooled, and your burned tongue spawned
small blisters as you wiped the black
smears from your mouth on your sleeve.

This is one story you told about the trek
across persecution and Europe
with your mother and four brothers.

And where you arrived as strangers,
to bless schools and work and enough food,
I call birthright and home. Now, we compost
and put out bottles and cans and never think
of the trash pickers who live beyond news.

Out of Light's Reach

Growing up, the Holocaust
was always on the edge
of my life, like fringe
on a prayer shawl,

or the eyes of wolves
in Jack London stories,
where prospectors huddled
close to a dying fire

with the hungry breath
and glowing desperation
of a nightmare waiting
just out of light's reach.

Baring the Common Burden

We knew no clinical name
for the way Ida walked
our streets, fitful as a robin
on a green, circling twice

before entering the house
she was there to clean.
We just knew the symptoms:
make-up that fit her

for Trick-or-Treat—orange face,
lipstick beyond the shape
of rationed expression,
melancholic trains of mascara,

and two bluebird eggs forever
peering out from behind blackout
curtains and dark expectation.
Brightly lacquered nails

were badly told lies on her
thick, rough-skinned hands. Her hair,
bleached yellow and dry, sprang
out and recoiled like Slinkies

of spooled barbed wire and shreds
of dangling skins a thousand serpents shed
to escape her concentration camped
in torment. She walked our street

dressed in our rumors and a man's
overcoat, the hem dragged
ragged-edged as the faded
yellow star sewn over her heart.

"Never forget!" she'd wail
pell-mell, tracing the star's
outline like a Christian crossing
herself. "For the kin'd'la.

Never forget!" She offered
candies children were warned
not to take, and pregnant women
lowered their eyes, lest they ingest

the curse of Ida's survivor gaze.
People hated her being there,
forcing their faces to the furnace
grating, baring the common

burden of man's genius for evil
and the limits of their own
compassion. People said
she poisoned pigeons in the park

at night. She'd sit on a bench
and read her *Daily Forward*
aloud, by candlelight, and sleep
with one hand over her star

and the other clutching a serrated
fish-cleaning knife. One night, two
policemen found her waving it
under a park lamp and dancing

in a granulated rainbow of fish
scales, sifting down a soup-thin
slice of light. She said it was glass
from shattered synagogue windows.

Imagine that. Imagine Ida walking
the strength of her labor and torment
down your street until it hurt to look
at her face: the black tears blistering

down to her clown-lipped mouth,
forcing hoarsely whispered words
into your ear, "We're only guests here.
Never forget! Never forget!" Who will

honor her memory where she danced
and kept her witness and covenant
alive, under the showering park lamp
where she hanged herself?

Light and Dark

The numbers on his mother's wrist hovered
beneath welts, like little blue fish in a red sea,
when he'd ask, "Why did God let Nazis kill
all the cousins, uncles, and aunts I never met?"

They peered up from beneath cuffs, holding
fast against blood's tide and memory. He still
remembers them glowing in TV light, and her
playing solitaire as if the numbers weren't there,

staring up at both of them. Bowed and numb, she turned
over the same thoughts until the shape of her thumb
worried through the pattern on the back of each card.
Then, when sun banded her blind-drawn heart,

like an artist's rendering of light and dark striping
a forest floor, she followed the care-worn path
between nightmare and dream to a pond shining
like a promise, a jewel of relief, where blue

gills rose like the clear, unblinking eyes
of conscience, and she slipped in with the ease
and buoyancy of a swimmer letting land go
to find a tide, to sleep.

Where Chemistry Fails

Because of the way men act in this world,
Primo Levi ran out of things to be
thankful for. But he never stopped loving
the way chemistry could explain how
things are made—that water is two parts
hydrogen and one of oxygen,
and stirring sunlight into that gaseous mix
makes the green brick-and-mortar of all life.

As a boy, that knowledge made him believe
one could know the world. Later, it saved him
from hard labor and death by another gas
at Auschwitz. But it could not explain why
men's brains, which are capable of composing
and appreciating a sonata, aspired to genocide.

Names for Home

You allow yourself one look back,
as if, like Lot's wife, you believed
you might gather once-in-a-lifetime
moments you lived there, gather them
up in your arms like a bouquet you
could carry away or place in a vase
on a window ablaze in yellow and blue.
Just last week, that was still true of your life.

But there is no place for bouquets
or last week in the frayed backpack
and bag you have taken to live in a subway
with your child. Beneath the reach
of bombs falling, sirens replace every
name you've ever known for home.

Bricks, Iron, Dust

after Zbigniew Herbert
and ending in lines from John Steinbeck

Is this the sum of Kyiv, Lviv?
Bricks? Iron? Dust?

Was this a street children walked to school?
Are these the sums they've been taught
division leads to?

This cap? This ponytail tie?
Where are these children?

O Mariupol. What is left
of your wheat fields waving like a sea in sunflower sun,
your Friday night cafes,
leaning in, elbows on candlelit tables?
Where are your aromatic kitchens,
the charm and gracious expanse of your boulevards?
What kingdoms!

Where is your skyline, Mariupol,
your window plants?

The moon shattering on water is illusion,
the Ukraine collapsing under map-coordinated
bombardments is cradle-to-mass-grave real.
Paper-donkeys will not run
because liars pin tails on one.

Is this is the sum of us: Bricks? Iron? Dust?
Human destiny is now in contest,
and nothing can be said as true:

"Yes, we are invaded. But I do not
believe that our people are conquered."

29

At the Center of Everything

I am near crying as I read
of a Russian mother reading
a letter from her son. He is
eighteen, in the army, in a convoy
heading for Kiev.

His first letter said they'd be welcomed,
cheered. This letter speaks of treachery
he's seen and what they've been ordered
to do to the men, women, and children
of Kiev. She fears it will ruin him.

I know she's right; there are places
in Vietnam that even now close my heart,
places where I discovered that you can live
on after your heart's stopped.

She knows he can't refuse the orders,
or he'll be shot. Or, if there is mercy,
he'll be jailed, like Galileo,
who also saw that our light was
not at the center of everything.

Everyday Memorial Day

Shot in the chest,
your body inadvertently
shielded me from death.

You fell back into water
over your head, your eyes open
but lifeless and far as two coins
staring up from the bottom of a well.

I knew my second wish,
and my first was already
true—it wasn't me.

We carried you out
and across the creek.
Dead, you were heavier than
in life. And that wish of mine,

heavier still. To this day,
I carry your death shrouded
in that wish, pronounced

in a restless silence that keeps
asking what more these hands
were spared to do? More than
five decades of asking,

and the question has grown
faint as the faint flower
of the moon in a blue

Memorial Day sky: I don't parade
it along Fifth Avenue or pose it
peering at my tearing reflection
from that black memorial wall,

but it's there, ever there,
thirsty and deep as any root
and still wanting an answer.

From the Wild

The hardwood floors were newly sanded, lacquered, and
    buffed to a low sheen.
The walls and ceiling were newly sheetrocked—one primer
    and two coats of paint
away from becoming the living room we had dreamed.

That's when the walls' monsoon gray ambushed me back to
    my first convoy
in Vietnam. It rained like I'd never known rain. Sergeant Lewis
    was riding dry
in the cab with the driver, Tom.

Fausto, Aidan, Jack, and me, the Fuckin' New Guy, were out
    in the rain on the flatback,
soaked cold and miserable. We were taking a prisoner from our
    firebase to headquarters
in Phu Bai. He was blindfolded, hands cuffed behind his back.

Fausto got up, ripped off the blindfold, and with his face right
    in the prisoner's,
screamed, "Fuck you!" Stepping back, he began shooting,
    "Fuck you! Fuck you!"
until he could see light and across the road through what had
    been the man's face.

I froze, my eyes seeking out the others. Jack shook his head,
    laughing,
Aidan repeated in a sing-song, "Fausto loco, Fausto loco!" I sat
    rigid, silent,
thinking, "There was no call for that."

No. No more reason for that than my picking up the crow bar
   and swinging
wildly, punching holes in the walls, pulling out chunks with the
   claw end,
until the peace I was so close to creating was destroyed.

I sat down and cried like a creature walled in by its own troweled
   up rage.
Then, I began to undo the damage before my family returned.
   If I had my way
No one would ever know what was behind that wall or what
   happened that afternoon.

Paco Sainte Sails Home

After the war, Paco Sainte built
ships in bottles and sailed away
in one each night. It wasn't long
before he discovered syringe
rockets could get him farther faster.

"It's just a place to go, where the war don't,"
Paco said. He wanted to forget the war,
the tides of blood, the ballistic
dismemberments of flesh. And he wanted
never again to be treated like a spic in America.

But he could not forget nor stop the dreams he had
or make true the ones he was denied. He lived
like a hooked fish, flipping about and slapping
out the last gasps of its life on the wood-board
bottom of a boat. So it comes as no surprise

that Paco washed up on a beach one night,
bottles broken, ships wrecked, all aboard dead.

Memorial Day 2021

for Easy

The brown splash and swirl in the glass.
I set down the bottle beside it,
the cork forced back in place. Any
smoky, sweet aromatic notes
that might escape would be wasted
on me, with tree pollen clogging
my sinuses. And if my eyes
are puffy and streaming tears, blame it
on that, too. But I snuck away
from friends who only think of this
as a long holiday weekend
before summer.

              For you and me,
it goes back to Quang Tri and a wet
mortar round that fell short of the LZ,
killed you and left me with a deadness
in the right ear that I thought had been blown off.
Blood on my hand when I reached for it
mistakenly confirmed that fear
and whatever else I might have lost
in that moment. I don't know that
we'd have remained friends, these fifty-two years
since. But I thought of you today,
as friends who are vaccinated gather
for a Memorial Day barbeque.

And this drink, I will drink alone,
throw it back all at once,
sudden as we were parted.

veterans day

skeleton-crowned trees
cannot recall holding

the leaves at their feet

though veterans rake
together their fallen

This is Not About You
(Not Being Afraid to Die)

When I heard him say, "I'm not afraid to die,"
I thought, he's never lived. Knowing I had

volunteered to go to war as a young man,
his parents ask me to speak with him.

I tell them it will make no difference,
but because I care about them, I do talk with him.

I tell him about war, which, as I expected,
makes him more eager, more enthusiastic,

even when I tell him that it never ends,
never leaves you alone. I know nothing,

as I told my friends, that could change his mind,
any more than anyone could have changed mine.

Finally, I tell him, "Go sit alone on a mountain top
for a few months before enlisting." "What?"

he asks, laughing. I say, "I suppose you don't
believe the world speaks to us, but it does, and it will

tell you that this is not about you not being afraid
to die; it is about you being afraid to live." "What?!"

Then, I went back and told my friends, his parents.
My friend, the mother, cried on the shoulder of my friend,

the father. Being a good man, doing what good men do
because they believe it's what good men do, he tried hard

to hold back his tears, just as soldiers do in war—one of many
small practices by which war teaches us to be inhuman.

For All Your Days

The past is never dead. It's not even past.
  William Faulkner

I am neither Hercules nor done with my labors,
yet serpents lay lifeless at my feet. I have killed
each one, yet they hiss and writhe alive in my mind,
for to witness war is to carry them for all your days.

When they escape their burlap confines, I recognize
the undying faces of the dead I've buried. How can
their faces still be so young! I grow old, gray, and wrinkled,
yet they remain forever the age that I was
when they were killed.

When they summon me, I go from wherever I am—
standing in a store aisle holding a tin of sardines
and a six-pack one year out, at work talking
across a desk with a colleague a decade later,
awakening in tears beside my wife in a new
century, or holding a pint at the bar, with one
foot up on the rest, my friends trying to pull me back
out of the long stare, but—
there I go, gone again.

I hate that serpentine hiss that's haunted me out
of sleep and peace for all my adult life, that's taught
my children to think of me as a disheveled, angry man
who flinches when a car backfires. I can wrestle
them back into their bag—the snakes, the faces, places,
and deeds, but even body-bagged and confined,
I never stop hearing or seeing them.

So know this to be true: enforce *the law of blood and death*,
and for all your days it will enshroud you as its keeper.

In an Election Year

Candidates dance in the court,
and their laughter echoes like coins
carelessly tossed down in cavernous,
marble-floored great rooms.

The wine there pours out a kind
of deliverance, while they pose,
waving from balconies and podiums.
And there are the picture-shows

of them with workers, listening,
shaking hands, open-collared,
willing to be a regular Joe,
as long as the cameras roll.

Their lips move in and out
of smiles, as if releasing birds
from between perfect teeth
with every hollowed-out word.

And as their yawping makes
headlines, the words of the news
slip off the page and along the floor,
like the letters in a thin alphabet

soup served in homeless shelters.
There, before those hungry doors,
and anywhere alms are needed,
each coin will stop its top-like turning

and return to pockets so deep,
many hands may fit, but few can reach.
And one morning, citizens, staring out
over coffee for a way to peace,

will read a trumpeting headline that one
king has proclaimed victory for all people,
under god. And those with jobs
will quietly get up and go to them.

All Our Glass Faces

There were more mass shootings in America
in the 2019 calendar year than there were days.
Gun Violence Archive

Mid-summer harvest. We await signs from Perseus,
amid another season of sloppy-sweet eating—licking peach
    syrup
and berry stains from our fingers and picking
    seeds and buttered corn skins
from between our teeth.

The night finds us out
late to watch meteor dust streak the space
of a blink aflame. We become effusively kid-like, shouting
    and pointing
at the stuff of our own brief spark and fire.

But out of some Dark Knight twist,
a young man whose mind writhes and whispers
like a bag of snakes enters through a theater exit,
equipped to shoot dozens of innocents.

Then, again, out of the solstice and child worship
of December, comes another frayed human to shoot out
elementary lives. Even unbridled child imaginations
could not shield them from what was about to happen.

And the shooters keep coming.
And the victims keep dying. And we glass-faced survivors
keep asking, as I did as a child,
when I first heard about Nazi death camps,

Why did God let it happen?

And for all the small-bore horrors since then, I add:
again and again and again and again. And

I still remember the first time my eyes were stung
by the sight of serial numbers on the soft veined
underside of wrists and arms. I thought they were seared on
by the molten-drip of branding irons used on cattle

in cowboy movies. But the numbers I saw
were impressed on human flesh, flesh of my flesh,
fellow Jews who I knew by name, at home, at school,
and at synagogue, where I soon after would abandon God ...

who still has not answered or intervened.

The Law of Peace, Work, and Health

Then, out from nature's purse and culture
of marshes, ponds, swamps, and trickles,
a toad swells to launch the first croak of spring.

And as if a report from a starter's gun,
it sends the entire earth within and without
to race and sing.

And if a bird calls from across a hollow,
and there is no one else to hear it, how shall I bear
such a small, lasting message of peace back to the world?

Perched Upon a Prayer

March cannot make up its mind.

Like mine, it is too mercurial

to stand on any one spit of mud

with the crow and the dove.

Its weathers are loud in contest

with my spirit, which bears the beat

and breath of any beautiful song

born in the throat of a bird,

perched upon a prayer.

So I asked: "April is there a place for me

amid your quickening and wings,

an open-armed embrace within

your crazed, expansive climate of faith?"

I waited for an answer in spring's

deafening busyness, where nothing could

hold still; least of all me. At last,

I said, "Alright then, I will meet you

where the fish sniffs at the hook.

Working

The ancient people of Newfoundland walked
winter's breath above and below frozen water,
moon, and starlight. At all hours, they believed
and cut holes as wide as their shoulders in ice.

When tides were out and the polished, muddy
bottom in sight, they'd slip under the ice crust
to gather clams and crabs and seaweed. Ever
on guard against the return of tide, they crawled
as if near the mud-spangled mouth of death. Out
and back, with only moonlight and ice to guide.

Reading of this ritual on a museum wall in Montreal,
freed from toil by a brief vacation, it seemed more
familiar than exotic—struggling for light and space
to seek sustenance and work against my own fears.

Day Labor

Here, morning lines up on corners.
Need brick work done, concrete?
Middle Easterners. That corner. Green market,
restaurant work? Mexicans. There. Poles
do good interior work, but take the Irish
for plumbing and electrical. That corner.

This is New York, drinking coffee in plain
blue paper cups at dawn. In every tongue,
the dream begins with showing up. Then,
your kids grow straight American teeth
and attitudes you will want to beat out of them,
but they'll read and write and never have to stand
on corners at dawn, waiting to be called names
and take grunt work no Americans want to do.

Restoration

for Soraya Hadasah Levine-Brooks

The cardinals on Myrtle Avenue sing
of spring as if nature belongs to its winged self,

despite the houses and concrete,
despite the cars lining alternate sides
of the street on alternate days

of the week. And every day it is so,
that people return from work and park

under power and telephone lines
with the Gabriel-like trumpeting
of cardinals singing *Cheer! Cheer! Cheer!*

as if welcoming them home,
as if restoring them to nature.

School Days

We invented language,
molded and rolled it
around the overheated room,
picking up ideas from every corner
with light, traffic sounds, and sirens

pouring reminders of the plain
world just outside, now decorated
red and green with stars
and possibilities for giving and love.

I could be one. Each of you,
another. Red and green.
Leaving for holiday, I pack
language and inventions we shaped,
history we made. All our fingerprints are there

Lost and Found Poetry

After watching the documentary about a poetry festival,
a student noticed the book on my desk, bearing the same title.
"Are all the poets from the movie in it?" she asked, picking it up.
"More," I said. "Would you like to read it? Take it."

Quick as those two words, her eyes widened. She placed one hand
on top of the book as if swearing an oath. Her smile broadened
to her eyes until I finished my thought.
"You can give it back to me after the holiday."

If the shades had been suddenly drawn and the lights turned off,
the room could not be more absent light than her face,
and I felt I was holding something broken
when she handed the book back to me.

Stink Street

What can be done for my anxious, asthmatic students
who carry my homework assignments home
down streets Dickens despised? They posture tough
enough to not be tried, picked on, or abused while
gasping for breath. Every day they care and struggle,
breathing lead and decay from the Bushwick air.

Bug spray- and frass-stink grab you by the nose,
throat, and lungs and won't let go. Like choke-hold
police, profiling and blind to the struggle and beauty
of street-crack daisies and sidewalk trees, muscling
up under street lights and broken-pane policies.
Don't they see Stink Street's children as children?
Don't they see that my breathless wards
are just kids? Damn it! They're *just* kids

Drawing Class

Railroad tracks are the classic
example to use if you're teaching
perspective in a drawing class.

Or you can stand your students
at one end of a street of buildings
of roughly the same size and shape—

brownstones, say, or projects.
But that can complicate the lesson
because buildings are in neighborhoods,

and neighborhoods make us think
words like good or bad, and students,
being only human, are bound to look

in the windows and up and down
the street and make judgments
about how well or poorly they think

people live where they live. Trust me:
if you want to teach perspective without
drawing class into it, stick to railroad tracks.

Against the Coming Heat

I'd gone in early to grade papers,
but Cal was waiting at my door with a box
of donuts. A thin, sugar-white mustache
powdered his upper lip. He sat on the floor so deep
in his despair, he didn't hear or notice me
until I said good morning, and then
he all but lunged to his feet, offering the box.

It was our class code, taken from a reading
in which African tribal manners dictated—
bring the host a gift, and never begin conversation
by discussing business. He remembered that
I'd had car trouble last week, so he asked about that,
then my family's health. By the time I'd put on
coffee and he'd opened the windows and lowered
the shades against the coming heat, we could hear
the schoolyard fill with voices, and we were ready
and got some things said, not resolved, but said.

That's when Shaniqua arrived with a mango.
Coming in too close, she held it under my nose,
talking too loud and too fast as she lit from one ledge
to another—the corner of my desk, the arm of my chair,
her seat, where she "wrote" on the desk with the clicker
of her pen, asking after my wife and my daughter,
who Shaniqua babysat when I brought her to class.
Then, like a wind-up doll run down,
she laid her head on her arms on the desk.

Cal tested me through the sequence of handshakes
I never got right and left me laughing, and the room reduced
to stillness against the schoolyard's increasing volume.
Shaniqua pretended to sleep. There is perhaps no quiet
quite like a classroom before classes begin. I drank it in
with my coffee, listening to the yard and Shaniqua's breathing
grow ragged. I knew when she raised her head, her voice
would be thick with tears and the lilting island accent she hid.
And just as I would later in reading the essays stacked on my desk,
I waited in practiced patience for a theme to emerge.

Walk the Walk

I called your orphan name,
and we walked together along
the long school street, dribbling
your rock across and back

between your legs as we talked.
"It's already too hot," I said.
"Too humid. Why're your eyes red?"
"Allergies," you sniffled.

I asked after your grandmother
and the days you'd missed.
"Allergies," you said.
I told you about the stray dog

I'd found. "Why people do
that, disown a dog?" you asked,
knowing about such things.
"Allergies," I said. "Oh!"

you laughed. "You played me!"
I shrugged. "See y'inside."
You prepared to drive the white
chain to the metal detector.

I could have taken you through,
as I did some mornings, but
suspected you were out
to let tempers cool, and even

now might feel the need for more
protection than I could offer.
Some days, you need to talk
and have learned that

I will listen. One day
you told me you didn't know
who your father was. Even
the window shades, lowered

like eyes, listened, wondering
which of us would speak next.
Thimble-thin thumps from your head-
phones counted time. No

such mystery today. All down
the hall to my room, I listened
to the alarm sounding like you
calling, "Yo! Mr. L!"

and feeling helpless
to help and knowing—feeling
for both of us—how thoroughly
your game was about to be shut down.

Like and Care

I think of her, of how, at first,
being kind seemed enough.

Though we didn't say it, we thought,
if forests grow from red-clover meadows,
why not love?

But like and care are not strong enough
to send down roots deep enough
or carry water far and high enough
to make them more than what they are.

And they are not love.

Whatever else love is, it is more
than like and care, more than wanting
to believe it is where it is not.

I tried. She did, too. And we were kind
until we hurt each other so thoroughly.

And that red-clover meadow,
where we first made love and laughed,
might be a mature forest by now.
But it never was ours.

The Round

"Lovers and madmen have such seething brains..."
William Shakespeare

Round
was her face, round as her
eyes, round as her cute, dimpled
buttocks, round, too, the way we talked
about what needed straight talk, straight talk
about our bad habits and how we cut corners
and the cutting ways we cornered each other, knowing
by heart how and where we hurt and the words that made
it better until the next go around, vowing no more well-
bottoms but just one more last time, one more
chance, O please, please, please—one more
round and lovely round together,
so good and bad and
round.

Skirt

Write just one sentence
to say you miss me the way irises
in the garden would miss flirting
with the single stalks staking them
to breeze and earth, irises with petals
as pale and delicately purple as the skirt
you wore the night I proposed,
and you accepted, and we eloped,

fierce and mild as bats and fireflies
divining the dark, as if it might be
the only life they'd ever have and their flight
a one-sentence sonnet to live and recite:
"O! I will miss that night,
the irises, their stalks, that skirt."

Foreplay

"She moves when time is shy:
Love has a thing to do."
    Theodore Roethke

All day I will carry this morning image:
her efficient hands fastening bra clasps
just under her slant-rhymed breasts.

I tie my tie as she slides the sheer flesh-
colored fabric cups around in one
two-handed sweep that covers the lovely,
bobbling, and pink-eyed nipples
staring back at me.

Standing in the mirror to dress with this
irony of urges, for flesh and work, she talks
itinerary and lists, while I half-kiddingly

insist on pleasure first. But she keeps us
to purposeful gestures until we've dressed
our reflections: I button down my collar
as she raises her arms over her head,

slipping into a white blouse, and with one
hand on my shoulder, steps into a skirt.
All day, amid the subway's strange

intimacy of strangers and the cubicle
contests of corporate stations,
I will carry this morning image of flesh
and good fortune until civil twilight.

Lullaby

All morning, a melody has insisted
its place in my thoughts, like the wind
stirring in tree crowns outside my window.

It is strong enough to turn birds
back from their desired compass,
and yet its comforts and lessons

are true in any language. How else
can we know the wind
and its voice but for the trees

and the birds and our own whistling?
And just so, when night draws its shade
on the children tucked in, it may be me,

droopy-eyed and mouthing a hypnotic
story-time verse, who is the first one asleep,
curled up fetal-like in the silences

between lullaby rhymes. Find me there, snug
under blankets of dreams and the morning
song that all day waited its turn to sing.

Reading to My Children

for Sonia Elizabeth and Emily Alice

My voice, trailing bright
pebbles, led us through
fairy-tale forests. You sat on
my knee, a raindrop on a leaf.

Sometimes, the moon loomed
close, knitting moths and cricket
songs to the screen. Trees listened
in their shadow-deep crowns,
like a council of kings seated

round the tall grasses of sleep and dream,
leaning in with the wriggling wind,
and everywhere approaching.
Even snow pressed its crystal

ears to our window, in turn, its soft,
curious insistence, "And then?
And then?" And if a cloud moved,
we said it was written. How I
treasured being there to read

to you, though it was too late
for me to believe in forever
or think we could
find our way back.

Fathers Playing Catch with Sons

after Donald Hall

In the yard with bat, ball, and mitt,
an athletic father and an artistic son
catch and throw misgivings. I played
for his favor and affection,
fearing even more than line drives,
the unmet expectation in his eyes.

Call it a measure of distance,
his disappointment and the gap
between home plate and the pitcher's mound.
Even now, with him long gone, that look
calls me out. I've kept it from my kids,
those felt but unshed tears and the sound
of grunted breath that filled the inch-wide
chasms between a swing and a miss.

Hourglass

This morning, I watched a father draw his son
in a wagon while their dog bounded about.
The day was young, bright, and cold.
I was on my way out of the park
when they entered. I stopped
to watch them play
a while, then
turned back
to my
life,
their joy
waning every
step, as my daughters
grow away from young mornings
of dogs and parks and innocence, warm
as a quilt tucked comfortingly about knees,
a veneer of safety and trust we held in mutual
esteem for as long as we and the world allowed. Still,
we are drawn on by generations and the stories we live.

Light

on holding my first grandchild for the first time on Fathers' Day

I hold you as if handed an egg
but what broke between us was light

light that rides the rail
that sets all life in motion
between two stations

What more might
might be asked of a moment

More Light

I like the days that follow easy
as ceiling fan blades, guiding warm air
into gravity's arms, and that way
we find and turn each other. Days when,
though I'd welcome company, I'm content
as a heron alone on a log,
one leg tucked up while meditating
over a pond of fish and summer wine.

At any moment, that heron might
slowly unfold its miracle
of flight, and stir the hypnotic tide
of quiet surrounding us, until
all we want is what Goethe called
for with his dying breath "More light."

River of Days

Such a small difference, between forever and once.
   Richard Powers

The wind was strong enough
to make the trees creak with their bending,
and rain pelted me as I walked out to cut
onion tops as a garnish for the root vegetables
already roasting in the oven. I stopped to pick
daffodils, too, and the wind blew off my cap.

The wind-wild rain, with no slack in it,
cleared my head and whetted my thirst for the taste
of bourbon. Once inside, my mind and garden
variety nags rushed back in: Isn't this enough?
Doesn't this satisfy the days and seasons of your life
worked like soil? Look at you with your clothes soaked
through, hands full of greens and yellows, and your heart
leaping like a fish from this splendid river of days.

Lancing Language

My wife starts days now, puncturing
a finger with a spring-activated device.

Quik Stik is the product name, and that is far more
comforting to say than *rive*, *rend*, or *impale*.

Vocabulary matters when a calm, efficient young woman
arrives at our door to teach my wife how to *stab* herself.

Terminology and the plastic device, which is
the size and shape of a lip balm tube, hide

the *Stik's* lance. It makes a blood dot as small
as the period at the end of this sentence.

She doesn't see it at first, but when a red bubble
sprouts up through the skin on the tip

of her finger, she dabs with a narrow paper strip
that reads the speed at which her blood will clot.

Utilizing sterile medical terms helps us talk
about what we have to do, what we might lose,

and about what the red worry bead
on the tip of her finger will say today.

Undressing a Lover

Pulling at a cuff, he watches her hand
disappear, leaving the sleeve limp
as the one draped over the cast
that holds her shattered bones in place.

With more care than lust knows,
he exposes her flesh. Raising the empty-
sleeved blouse over her pained expression
leaves him momentarily alone.

Detaching hook from eye, one at a time,
he unclasps her bra from behind. Her breasts
droop out. Deliberately, his hands slip straps
over both her casted and unbroken arms.

She holds the bad with the good,
grimacing as he draws down her pajama pants
and panties. Then, in a realm only their passion
has known, and long ago stripped of shyness,

the mechanically strange intimacy
of a sponge bath makes them modest, awkward.
He touches her carefully, so as not to arouse pain.
And yet, their hearts break with each clinical embrace.

Winter Fires

for Sharon

Before we first kissed, there was a moment
we leaned into, like two birds in the instant
before flight. Our lips touched, and up we flew
over the coldest February night. Snow and ice
melted, eaves dripped, streams uncoiled,
and the woods rang with the hoots of mating owls.

All that way across loneliness to stars,
we testified, time and again, that yes,
there was such a night we are still devoted to.
Some terrible things happened and were endured,
and seasons were not the only changes.
And when we find ourselves in another spring
garden, we season the soil with ashes from winter
fires and seeds for new memories.

The Law of Endangered Environments, Viruses and Hope

"We have the world to live in on the condition that we will take good care of it. And to take good care of it, we have to know it. And to know it and to be willing to take care of it, we have to love it."

Wendell Berry

A Wood, Like a Poem

A wood, like a poem,
turns and turns: enchanted and real,
dream and waking, musical and mute,
shadow and light, body and soul, young and old,
beautiful and grotesque. In a wood, life and death nest
together in trees — yes, they are mostly trunk dead; beneath
their dwarfing poses they are little more than poles of cellulose
and lignin, driven to grow close to the sun to infuse chlorophyll,
muse of all things green and alive,   from crowns to ground cover.
Everything you can   discover in a wood you can uncover in a poem.
And, of course, a walk in a wood is always just a walk in a wood ... just that miracle.

1. From fields, where once cows, with their soft mouths and blunt herbivore teeth daily
disturbed all possibility of green but for grass, a forest in transition now scales the air, alive
with fruits, berries, nuts, and seeds, more shrubs, bushes and vines than trees; a stage of fores
birds and wildlife most love – less wood than food-lot. This instinctual love is undeterred b
the stanchioned bellows of cows, barn-bred and lamenting their exile from
the wild. 3. Walking in the climax forest the trunks and crowns are grown thick recording eac
chapter in the history of wind. Some topple or snap, but the standing speak to each other all nig
and sign by shadow all day. All day, repeating the oceanic tide of leaves into oospheric clods of e
clutched between the gnarled, incubating fingers of roots. 3. Every walk in nature is a walk into th
that lives patient as a fish, hanging low and still in the frozen slush of winter ponds, releasing it
increasingly slower beads of breath until spring, when it approaches the mirror and the unjamb
door between life and death, then leaps free, arcing into the universe of air, free from darknes
that is always there waiting its turn, free from the bones aching and ever more ill-fit in aging
flesh, free from the dark of thought and time and thoughts of time. 4. I deny the well-tread
trails walking instead the nest-like tangles and weaves where life is hatched;
and I feel at home, finding every where, every day, the woods I walk awake
in me thousands of tenacious lives and reasons to be attentive
at every turn. At every turn, something
is given. I stop and kneel, to watch a black
ant struggling along with an insect wing
clutched between its shiny mandibles.
When I rise, my own height makes me dizzy.
The wood's primordial madness of scale
and proportion explodes into my awareness,
freeing me,   suddenly,   as poem.

At Our Door

Seagulls fly inland when a storm approaches.
Ducks and geese and coots feed in pools
where ice has not yet stitched its cold knits and purls.

Nails I drove to fast lintels and tongue-and-groove
ceiling boards to the roof's frame now feel
a force testing their hold and send long shivers

through the length of joists they call home.
I hear their rusty, arthritic creak holding on,
as if the wind had teeth to gnaw

and hands to push and pull and drum
and rip windows from walls and set
the whole house humming like a hornet's nest.

My life and home stand confident
as I have made and maintain them
with my own hands. But beyond

my reach are the four seasons
and the hinges and doors between them,
and we can all see how they have begun

to swing out of kilter with bees
and migrations, moon-tides and stars.
And under my skin, like a child

tucked in, warm and listening
to *The Three Little Pigs*,
I quake at what appears to be at our door.

Delicately Boned Hope

Noah, so the story goes, stood in the bow
of despair, his brow broad with wonder
at the delicately boned hope he'd released,
to find a dry light in the flood-sluiced dark.

It's a story, after all, of a man. But how
can the secular see him, except as delusional:
he hears voices! One, at least, pours down
torrents about carpentry and the consequences

for man's continued defiling of creation.
Still, even now, it's quite a story. After all,
who would not be afraid of the signs: flooding,
endless rain, rising seas, wildfires, holes in the sky?

The Limits of Science

You can count strata in a quarry,
ages of hunger we still know,
thousands of years of struggle packed
tight in a few inches of stone.

Doesn't look like our history, though.
Just a layer cake of rock to an untrained eye.
But scientists say they see us—
then, now, tomorrow, in colors

and compression. They say they don't need
to look beyond the rings of trees,
being clear-cut or dispossessed
by mountain-top mining,

to tell us why climate is changing faster
than we can adapt. But they can't point
to a layer and say, *here* is where greed
overwhelmed reason, and *there* is where

we failed to be kind and take the time
to understand in lieu of genocide.

Our Turn

The U.S. Fish and Wildlife Service is proposing to remove 23 species
from the Endangered Species Act due to extinction—the most ever
at one time.
    Reuters, September 29, 2021

Perhaps, if we had to attend a funeral
for each species on the day it becomes extinct—
each of us having to prepare a eulogy to read—

perhaps then, we'd learn.

Perhaps, if we heard the unraveling
of the rope suspending the cathedral bell
above us as we spoke our mournful words,

perhaps then, we'd quake.

Perhaps, if leaves and wind could teach
us to sing the songs in autumn's hymnal,
we might hear how each whirligig descent
from being means one less voice lightening
our loneliness—

perhaps then, we'd pause to listen.

Or, perhaps, it's too damn late for us to see
through the latte steam, the increasing number
of missing pieces in the chain of life we're linked to,
as sure as the drive-thru queue we are waiting on,
wondering how close it is to our turn.

The Waterfall Roar

Leaves of grass had never known
the scent of combustion engine gas
curling on the air or Molotov rain
inflaming the earth and our lungs,
had never known the infatuation
that overcame us, summoning wind
anytime, anywhere, to comb our hair
with speed, as we raced along roads,

squushing insects against the shield
of our ignorance, the winding, speeding
future of being in our hands, wheeling ahead
of death, just around every bend, careening,
racing, fast and faster, more and more,
the waterfall roar close and closer.

Hocus-Pocus

What if, like light from dead stars,
the forests we see are already gone?

We know there are fewer birds and bees
to pollinate, fewer rabbits to hunt

or pull out of hats. Can it be
we are just one generation of seeds

away from becoming a magician
who gets caught in his own trick?

What incantation or wave of a wand
can save us then? What old hocus-pocus

must be said or done before it's—
Now you see us, now you don't!

Atonement

In my struggle to learn a minuet in G,
I wonder about its Benedictine
composer, a monk who meditated

and played lute by the hour
in a seventeenth-century monastery.
He may have been a man of faith

or a gifted child sent forth to sooth
a streak of wild. As my fingers
clumsily pronounce sacred moments

he composed, do I seem closer to God,
more angelic, less likely to do again
the harms I have done? As atonement

for misplaying a tone meant as a grace
note, I stop to understand how I have
corrupted my time. The metronome's

slow trimeter reconciles my hands
to breath, so the notes cease to be
a series of desperate hopes but sing

free and loud as banjoes and ducks,
and it undoes me long enough
to forget what's still left undone.

Light and Life

Perseus was shrouded in cloud
when I walked out to watch an hour
pass, like a disciple who'd left
his life behind for such a night.

I had abandoned delights
of touch and sound to stand bereft
of those senses and chance the fall
of hourglass sand on fire. The vault

of stars hid from my eyes, till, deft
as a prayer answered, clouds parted.
Then, I saw loneliness alive
in my heart. But, as if by theft

and quick as a pocket picked,
streaks of light and life arrived as gifts.

Civil Twilight

A train passes on the outskirts of town
as I step outside my house, for the fragrance
of clover and milkweed. Scent is as invisible
as a distant train and its whistle, or a mourning
dove's coo from the leaf-thick crown of a nearby tree.

It is late August, and all day rain has sent slow-
moving clouds and breathlessly humid air to say
I am on my way with relief for the parched green
and parturient earth. Now, at dusk, it comes. At first,
softly as a radio heard from an approaching car.

I stand in the light rain until it gathers the force
to rinse the sweet from civil twilight. The train
whistle blows again, and I go inside to tell my wife
this latest from the world. On the news, police
shoot an unarmed black man, again and again.

Is!

in memoriam, Joe Hayman

I had gone to take the bare trees of my thoughts to walk
in the park, seeking consolation in goose honks, coot dives,
the lily-white of swans beneath the ominous
red-tailed glide of a hawk and the small talk of a sidewalk
bush, alive with dozens of chirping sparrows.
Dozens. Chirping. For today, I was bound to bear
my heart like sad hands hiding in shallow pockets.

Since the news, grief has collected and disquieted
memories tangled like fish lines, sticky, blood-barbed hooks,
sinkers, snares, bobbers, and bones,
all thrown in and cast to rattle a racket in a gray pail,
where the stink's cooked in and as sharply pronounced
as the cacophonous, sad-handed carrying of it.

To no avail, I am parading in grave-muddy boots,
as if passing like a clarion every hearth where our names
are known and called is helpful—Am! Are! Is!
Damned present tense!
Dear friends, our superlatives are but a palliative ruse,
for we have gathered today to past tense our friend's every verb,
pull out each one like a dead fish from a bucket.

What, but an inevitable occupation.
Tis true, tis pity; tis pity, tis true.

But come, cast each in his chowder pot and gather edible nouns—
fish heads first, then turnips and beans, parsnips and greens,
coriander and fenugreek, for a stew he'd simmer all day
to shut winter's windows and doors against itself,
because gray is a lonely ache.
Is! Again!

Here! Give a stir, as he did, humming arias and songs
over the stewing pot, maybe "In Tarbena Quando Sumus"
or "Lydia the Tattooed Lady." And open plenty of wine bottles
for the long nights and the cold heave.

And come, call on every creature to sing
for a dear friend, a sweet choir voice, which first rose
in the building of ricks under barn lofts and weather-vane skies.
And that boy, that hay-man boy who would one day want to feed
and sing for everyone he knew—for he knew how we were
all always so hungry and what for—
that fine fellow, my dear friend, is dead, is no more is.

Listen, as I was telling you,
this morning, as I wandered the park,
my bare tree thoughts encaged a hawk
not twenty feet above where I stood.
In its thrall, I watched the graceful swivel
of its head and eyes, its bullet body
as still and hard as its raptor beak.
But its feathered majesty could not fool me,
not today; I know what its swift,
hollow-boned villainy is here to undo.
Is! Is!

cOVID's Metamorphosis

1. *Blessing Our Hands*

As if water were holy,
as if our hands were miracles
we have just discovered
and learned to love and awe,
we wash them after touching
the world.

In rolling caresses,
intertwining fingers, nails,
and knuckles, they work soap
into a lather with light from dead stars.

It is a simple baptism
our mothers first performed for us.
We have continued its practice, forgetting,
perhaps, the insistence of love
as we squirmed to escape.

In our now threatened lives,
the import of washing our hands
has outgrown its innocent,
merely functional purpose,
like snails their shells, like snakes their skins,
like our baby selves
the amniotic embraces
our mothers gave.

So we practice this
simple ritual to purify our hands
against galaxies of lethal taint
our eyes fail to see
while the faucet sings in the key
of oceans and runnels, pouring forth,
whispering all and ever.

But even washing and believing
in the beauty of our hands
cannot grace us with immunity
from the jellyfish sting of fear.

Passing my masked and unmasked
neighbors on the same earthly streets
we strolled so carelessly yesterday,
I nod, my eyes smiling bravely.

2. Sheltered in Place

for Quitman and Marcel

You watch your boy struggle with giving
up the turtle crossing his palm, returning
it to the pond where he'd found it on a walk—
first time you'd all been out in days.

How thoughtful he thought he'd been,
making it a home in the home
where the family sheltered in place.
How he cared for his armored friend.

Having picked flowers, knowing they'd die,
you understand the urge to pluck
the exotic, the beautiful—any diversion
from fear, which is in itself a disease.

That morning, donning masks, you helped your boy
give up the idea of living forever.

3. Confined

after Rainer Maria Rilke's "Panther"

Confined within walls of days, and all my days
are all the same walls. I have memorized
each one, like a menu from a café
or diner I used to go to among friends.

Now, I can only stalk such thoughts around,
circling my cramped, right-angled apartment,
where each wall becomes one thousand and one
bars, caging me in with no world beyond contagion.

"Only at times, the curtain of my eyes lifts
and an image enters" my walled-in heart,
which I fear of late has become a place
where vision goes to die. But soon, it might again

know what parachutes know—the rush from cramped
rucksack confines, the thumping open at beauty
or a blue sky. And then, it might remember my simple
tastes: I just want to go out to a movie

and then talk about it over a few pints
or shop in a store, picking out my own
produce, and walk home unmasked, unafraid,
and able to see and look into every face.

4. Trespassers Will

The world once fit and protected
us, like these face coverings we wear
now to armor ourselves against it.
O Mother, have you abandoned us?

You were so beautifully at peace
until we cut down your trees to farm
and carved diamonds from your veins
to make our finger rings sparkle.

Now, the fox has nowhere to run,
the deer, raccoons and bears all
come closer, though there is nothing
older than their fear of our ways.

Cowering at home, we feel homeless,
coveting the lives we led without
the hungry virus roaming our empty streets,
its snout steaming contagion.

5. Contagion

"The weariness, the fever and the fret ...
Where palsy shakes a few sad, last grey hairs."
    John Keats

We keep to the newly prescribed
physical distancing when in
store lines, survival purchases
in our plastic, blue-gloved hands.

Floating above our masks, our eyes
give us away. Every expression
of doubt or fear becomes a tome
we all read and feel. We look tough

as eggshells, six feet apart, twelve
to a box we dare not drop. Time
slows to an intravenous drip.
Our eyes bear so much, floating

hope above our masks, and this tide
of contagion raging around our lifeboat.

6. Who Made the World

for CG

The phone rang, as smartphones ring.
Even COVID-19 could not change that.
A friend said a friend was dead,
but my thoughts embraced his wife—
barred from visiting, unable
to say a last face-to-face goodbye
before the eternity without him.
In quarantine and loneliness, I grieved.

I held the phone, looking at it
as if there must be more to tell,
something more caught in digital
synapses between yes and no, between
then and now, between zero and one,
who made the world bearable.

When You Find Clover

When you find clover and milkweed
floating on the night, as your sight
measures your standing in the world
to the farthest Milky Way star,

it's like hearing a voice you'd beg
on your knees to keep on hearing
as long as you live. Maybe it's the voice
Moses and other prophets heard.

Here and now, no voice, no prophets,
just me and this blessing of being
a man out to walk in the night.
And, as if from a trance, the earth

shakes me, breathing a life-awakening
fragrance into my nostrils.

Everything Is Fine

It is autumn. Leaves fall like slow rain,
slower and seemingly lighter than air,
but gravity proves itself with every leaf.

On the ground, they begin the process
of not being leaves. Decomposition
composes them into a new organic galaxy

that explodes and composts the universe,
faster than mountains grow but slower
than rain falls. People love to watch

this metamorphosis, though it makes them
melancholy. Would it surprise you to learn
that couples break up more often in this season?

I'm just asking. Everything is fine at home.
Really. It is autumn. Leaves are falling.

This Stirring

for Al Rizzo

There is this stirring
in my head and a nest
near the top

of the sidewalk sycamore
outside my window.
Its leaves turn to wings

on fire for one flight
that sweeps rasping old men
into red-cheeked usefulness.

Under dogwoods gone
burgundy, they work
with straw brooms, gossip

and memory, mixing
cigar smoke and stinking
ginkgo fruit with the pinched-

nosed screams of children
running up and down
the street. It is autumn,

and up and down the street,
there is this stirring.

Thanksgiving Day

              I wake at dawn,
blinking into this universe
called life.
              I could be just
a scattering of moments,
a pestering
              cloud of May flies,
a fluorescence of wild mushrooms
huddled along
              a hiking trail
for just one day, or stars clustered
round a force
              strong as my love.
But this being Thanksgiving Day,
I breathe a small
              breath, say these words
and your names as blessings to count,
and bow my head.

Upon My Soul

with a line from Donald Culross Peattie

It is the flowerlessness of winter,
the birdlessness of it, that makes me feel

more than cold. The wind moans, and then,
as if fearing that its own admission

of loneliness might make it appear weak,
it howls and roars, rattles windows, finds the creak

in walls and trees; all to say this wilderness is wild
and in winter dark and hollow.

This is what I say, too, missing the nod
and soft consoling sigh of leaves. For all

my walking in winter's woods—following
tracks to where they stop and scratch

for the cartography of songs and wings
and mating and some wit of insect or green—

I am always longing to come upon my soul,
which only shows me what a cane tapping

lets a blind man know of the world. Yet, with no song-
bird or flower to be found in the kingdom of cold,

where mud speaks of ice to bone
and even tree sap has withdrawn to root,

the candle on our table, where we sit to eat,
tells one truth about what light may bring.

Remember the Birds

Remember the birds read the poles
and shape a geometric equation
where time and distance equal
a season of chalk skies.

Remember the frosted warble
from the cusp of intersecting lines
and the promise of warm seasons
that come and go on wings.

Remember you wanted to go
the distance they travel to silence,
leaving nothing but bricks and bones
and the charcoal sketches of chimneys.

Remember, on the coldest day,
when the visible world is a quilted blank page,
remember song birds read the poles
and return in magnetic motion.

So It Is Today

One can give nothing whatever without giving oneself.
  James Baldwin

for former president Barrack Hussein Obama

Lincoln's statue stands so tall and straight,
so sad-faced, as if even in stone, he knows
the Civil War is still in contest.

Looking at him, looking over the new
rink in Prospect Park, as if thinking

through the falling snow to Grand
Army Plaza, where standing stone

soldiers he sent to save the Union
still raise the flag, guarded by angels

and apocalyptic steeds that rear
under an ever-embattled sky.

Today, a Black president sits
in the White House. Outside, he will place

a wreath at the stone feet of Abraham Lincoln.
So it is, today. So it is.

Now in Contest

I sometimes fear
my last thought
may be of me
soldiering in Vietnam.
1967 or eight.

I want that last breath
retreating behind my terminally closed eyes
to be of me with my wife, my kids, my pets,
or anywhere anytime
I was kinder in my life.

Everyday

Thanks, Buddy Holly, for rhyming
"gettin' closer" with "roller coaster"

and for making us believe songs
and love would "surely come our way."

And thanks, too, for the guitars and harmonies
in sync with the cricket-pulse in our thighs

and for singing the hiccupping ache and twang
of yearning summer nights, "A-hey, a-hey-hey."

Acknowledgments

Abandoned Mine "Paco Sainte Sails Home"

Adirondack Review "Perched on a Prayer"

Alembic "Bahbe," "Restoration"

American Life in Poetry "Sheltered in Place"

A Ritual We Read to Each Other (anthology) "School Days"

Baseball Bard "Fathers Playing Catch with Sons"

BigCityLit "Hocus-Pocus," "Light and Dark," "Like and Care," "Wade in the Water"

Black Moon Magazine "Undressing a Lover"

Chaffin Journal "Lullaby," "Where Chemistry Fails"

Comstock Review "Blessing Our Hands"

Connecticut Poetry Society Award "Is!"

Counterpunch "Memorial Day 2021"

Cross-Cultural Communications "Drawing Class"

Evening Street Press "The Limits of Science," "This is Not About You (Not Being Afraid to Die)"

Invasion of Ukraine: 2022 "At the Center of Everything"

Main Street Rag "Confined," "Everyday," "Thanksgiving Day"

More Than a Memory (Vietnam anthology) "Everyday Memorial Day"

Mudfish "At Our Door"

North Dakota Quarterly "Working"

October Hill Magazine "Light"

Slab Lit Mag "Every Day, You Say," "Trespassers Will"

So It Goes "Contagion," "Who Made the World"

Stories That Need to be Told (anthology) "Fat Pickers"

The Orchard Poetry Review "Light and Life"

The Practice of Peace (anthology) "Hourglass"

The Same "Reading to My Children"

Shrew "Skirt," "The Round"

VerseWrights "Atonement," "Lost and Found Poetry"

Vox Populi "Day Labor," "More Light," "One Night in America"

Westchester Review "Names for Home"

Young Ravens Review "Upon My Soul," "When You Find Clover"

Title Index

D

E

F

H

I

L

M

N

O

P

R

S

T

First Line Index

W

Y

CPSIA information can be obtained
at www.ICGtesting.com
Printed in the USA
JSHW031605150723
44805JS00004B/213